10
FEAR LESS
DO MORE
LESSONS

*On Your Journey
to Fulfill Your Dreams*

TAMMY ADELE WILLIAMS

Copyright © 2022 by Tammy'Dele Publishing

All rights reserved. This book, or any portion thereof, may not be reproduced or used in any manner whatsoever without the express written permission of the publisher except for the use of brief quotations in a book review.

Printed in the United States of America

Cover Design by Madison McPeters & Adele

Illustrations by Keystrm

First Printing, 2025

ISBN: 978-0-9669254-4-9

Tammy'Dele Publishing

145 Robinson Drive

Fayetteville, Georgia 30214

www.TammyDelePublishing.com

This book is lovingly dedicated to those who are ready to turn their words into action and their dreams into reality.

SPECIAL THANKS

To all who played a role, big or small, in bringing this book to life, I appreciate you more than words can express. Thank you!

A heartfelt gratitude to the game changers in my life- Alvin Williams, Terence Johnson, my extended family, and a host of friends— my tribe. Thank you for always inspiring me to dream forward.

A very special thank you to my Mom, my greatest cheerleader, whose love and support continues to uplift me, even in her absence.✝ I am the hairdresser's daughter.

TABLE OF CONTENTS

INTRODUCTION	1
POWER POINT 1 **_IDENTIFY YOUR FEAR HABIT_**	3
POWER POINT 2 **_THE COMFORT ZONE_**	7
POWER POINT 3 **_EATING ALONE_**	10
POWER POINT 4 **_SERVE IT UP_**	14
POWER POINT 5 **_WHEN NOBODY KNOWS YOUR NAME_**	17
POWER POINT 6 **_ONE STEP_**	19
POWER POINT 7 **_GOOD SUPPORT_**	22
POWER POINT 8 **_FOCUS FORWARD_**	25
POWER POINT 9 **_BE TEACHABLE_**	28
POWER POINT 10 **_SEE IT. BELIEVE IT. DO IT._**	31
FINAL WORDS	34
REFERENCES	38

"I survived because the fire inside me burned brighter than the fire around me."

Joshua Graham, a character in the action role-playing game, Fallout: New Vegas

Introduction

On your journey to fulfill your dreams, imagine how much more you could do with a bit more confidence and a little less fear.

Fear, often labeled as the ultimate procrastinator and the biggest dream destroyer, stands as a barrier in the journey of life. It can hold us back from pursuing our passions and achieving our goals, making it one of the toughest challenges we face on our path to success.

How do we fear less to do more?

You have the power and ability to move forward despite circumstances rooted in fear of rejection or failure. Confronting these fears is the first step in the Game Changer Playbook. It is the start of your next level - new normal.

I have worked in the film and television industry for over 30 years and am still very passionate about the work I do. However, there are times when I have found myself in fear, especially when taking on something out of my comfort zone. Over the years, my fearless lifestyle has leveled up—I'm rising higher every day. I have learned different strategies to overcome situational fear. It has not always been easy, but it *has* been rewarding!

On this journey to fulfill my dreams, I have met, worked, and learned from many amazing professionals in the business. Here are 10 fear-less/do-more lessons. Be sure to review these principles again and again.

Fear can be relentless, but so can Confidence!

POWER POINT

1

IDENTIFY YOUR FEAR HABIT

A *stunt performer* is someone who performs dangerous stunts in a film or television production in place of an actor (*Collins Dictionary*). Stunts include fighting, jumping off buildings, precision car driving, etc.

Through the years, I've met a few well-known stuntmen, and some of them have the same baffling confession: they are afraid of heights. I was curious to know how a stunt performer could be afraid of heights. How can a person effectively complete a job he is afraid of? They all had the same answer; "I just do it." Do it in spite of the fear.

Sometimes we wait for the perfect moment and for all our ducks to be in a perfect row before even attempting to start what we know deep inside what we need to do. First, fear tells you to wait. When you wait, fear comes again and says, "It's too late; you missed it." You just got played. Fear has played the ultimate setup. The goal is to get you so delayed, that you quit.

When I was a kid, we would play "Mother, May I?" When asked by the leader to take a step or spin, you had to ask for permission first, "Mother, May I?" and wait for the leader's response, "Yes, you may." Then, and only then, could you make your next move. However, if you did not ask for permission and moved first, you had to start all over again. Another strategy that fear uses is making you think you have to wait for permission to follow your dream. We search for a leader to say, "You can do it." I am not saying that you don't need wise counsel as having mentors is important. What I'm referring to is getting permission to live. No one has to say, "It's okay to breathe now." It comes automatically; you just do it.

Identify how fear influences your self-expression.

How do you react to fear when it attacks? Getting to know you is the greatest networking you can do. I've always wanted to produce. Organization and creative producing are comfortable spaces for me. I directed talent in commercials, but never a narrative feature. When I was approached about directing a feature film, my response was that of avoidance. It was like I kept delaying getting back to the person that asked. This is how my mind, soul, and body reacted to something I had never done before. I stepped back, saw how this behavior played out in other situations, and realized I had to deal with it. I took a giant leap and stepped into it. I am so glad I did. Many of the skills I had learned in directing commercials came into play, and yes, mistakes were made, but it widened my path as I discovered another great joy in my life: directing. I got a chance to see something develop inside of me. There are so many hidden jewels inside of you. Imagine what you could do if fear wasn't hugging you.

ACTION ITEM: Think of one thing you fear and do it first.

CONFESSION: Things I fear, I do them first.

Knock it out and get it off your mind.

POWER POINT
2
THE COMFORT ZONE

A *screenwriter* is someone who writes screenplays

It is extremely important for writers to find an environment that makes them feel comfortable and relaxed in order to do their best work.

Whether you are working 9-5 for a company or are an entrepreneur with infinite hours, finding the right space to thrive aids your success.

When an environment is no longer conducive for growth, change your environment, or the environment will change you. Toxicity stunts Creativity. Here's a caterpillar-to-butterfly example. As the caterpillar transforms into the butterfly, the butterfly must break the outer layer of the cocoon in order to fly. The environment that was once helpful turns harmful if the butterfly stays. In order to be all that it can be, it must leave the safety of the cocoon, moreover, the process of emerging is essential for its survival and health.

Baby birds leave the nest when they reach the fledging stage, a point in their development that varies depending on their species. However, a mother bird may encourage the baby to leave by lessening the frequency of food brought to the nest. For a moment, imagine a baby bird growing into a full adult bird still sitting in the nest her mom built, never learning to spread her wings. Simply sitting with her head back and mouth open, waiting for the mother bird to stuff food down her throat. If you want to go and grow, avoid staying too long in your comfort zone.

As the saying goes, you don't have to go home, but you need to get the heck up outta here.

> **ACTION ITEM:** Evaluate your current environment; are you growing, stagnated, or evaporating?
>
> **CONFESSION:** Change is not change until I change.

If growing, keep learning new skills and taking on challenges to continue moving forward.

If you feel stagnated, figure out what's holding you back, ask for advice, and try new ways to improve.

If it seems as though you are evaporating or on a downward spin, be flexible by learning new things, meeting new people, and exploring different job options.

POWER POINT
3
EATING ALONE

"A *caterer* is a professional or business that specializes in providing food and beverage services for events, gatherings, or occasions.

One of the many things I love about working on set is the food-from snacks at crafty to delicious entrees at catering.

Great caterers have a real sense of people. They are patient and have an innate kindness. It takes those attributes to work with customers when a basic need must be met in a timely manner.

Great caterers take pride in their food. They want customers to have not just a meal, but an experience. They know what foods work best together to bring out the best flavors and how it all should be arranged visually. Their "why" must be strong enough to carry them through even the toughest of critics. Even the best caterers know that even when they have done their best, everyone is not going to like everything.

On your journey to fulfill your dreams, you must be hungry (pun intended) or passionate enough about your dreams that you're able to stand when others don't understand. Like a great caterer, you must continue to work even if someone does not like everything on the plate.

Secondly, see people in 3D. Seeing people as whole, complex individuals helps build stronger connections and better understanding, while oversimplifying them limits relationships and empathy. It's about changing how you think to appreciate people for who they really are.

Meet people where they are versus where you want them to be.

Thirdly, try those green eggs and ham, you might just like them.

Be willing to try new things. Moreover, don't run away from something because it looks different or it's unfamiliar. Step into it with both feet!

Fourthly, be kind to everyone regardless of status, wealth, or power. How one treats those who are vulnerable, marginalized, or in need (the least of these) says a lot about one's character. Moreover, The least of these today can be your boss tomorrow.

Fifthly, like the caterer, be confident in your strengths and what you bring to a project. See yourself as the game changer.

Know what you bring to the table and don't be afraid to eat alone. You will have visions and dreams that even those closest to you will not always see. Some will see it immediately. Some will see it when it's complete and others never will. Nevertheless, the important thing is that you see it. Understand your value.

The person who can confidently eat alone, i.e. stand on business is one to be admired.

ACTION ITEM: Write down three of your greatest strengths.

CONFESSION: I know what I bring to the table, and I'm not afraid to eat alone.

POWER POINT
4

SERVE IT UP

A *production assistant* is a member of a film or television crew that performs entry-level tasks such as answering phones and running errands.

The production assistant on a film or television set is considered the lowest position on the production totem pole. However, one cannot make a great film without a great PA. A good PA's mindset is one of service; "What can I do to help move this production forward?" A great PA equals great support. Great support equals promotion. The wise PA knows and understands this is a learning position and takes full advantage of the moment.

As a PA, I learned that if you're willing to wait, you won't be waiting for long. Moreover, grow where you're planted. Maximize the time and never despise small beginnings. See, a PA already possesses greatness on the inside. She is now in a season of cultivation and waiting for the education to meet the opportunity.

When starting a new position, a new project, or doing something you've never done before, one may feel like a PA. Trust me when I tell you, once you learn the ropes, it's game on! While you're learning, maximize the moment by taking one step at a time, leaving no stone unturned.

There is something about knowing who you are and what you're made of that you don't mind doing the small things to help people get bigger. Great leaders serve. We all have the potential to be great leaders. Dr. Martin Luther King Jr. said, "He who is greatest among you shall be a servant. That's a new definition of greatness. By giving that definition of greatness, it means that everybody can be great because everybody can serve." Serving does not mean operating as a doormat. It's growing others while you are growing. Eventually, those seeds of service will come back to you, when you need them the most.

ACTION ITEM: Today, serve someone. Help with the small things.

CONFESSION: I am a great servant leader.

POWER POINT
5

WHEN NOBODY KNOWS YOUR NAME

A *background actor*, or *extra*, is a performer in a film, television show, stage, musical, opera, or ballet production, who appears in a nonspeaking or silent capacity, usually in the background.

Background actors fill a void. They make a scene more real while at the same time being unnoticed. They cannot outshine the lead actors.

Your dream will fill a void. It is the answer to a very real problem. There are people waiting for you to step into your purpose. When Harriett Tubman took on the task of helping free slaves, first, she filled a void.

Secondly, there were people waiting for her to take her position in the Underground Railroad. In the end, she helped many slaves start new beginnings. Good leaders know how to lead and how to be in the background when necessary. They understand the strength of both. Don't worry if no one knows your name. Don't discount or despise small beginnings. Your time will come. When God makes your name great, you never have to worry about your fame fading.

People may not see you coming, but they'll know when you get there.

ACTION ITEM: Today, talk only when required. Practice listening and watch how much you learn by being in the background.

CONFESSION: I'm operating in my area of influence. Within me, is the answer to a problem.

POWER POINT
6
ONE STEP

A *choreographer* is someone who invents the movements for a dance and tells the dancers how to perform them.

The choreographer can take a group of untrained dancers with a bad routine and bring them in sync, one step at a time. I watched this dance show called *So You Think You Can Dance*. It was intriguing watching a good dancer turn great in a matter of weeks. However, one of my favorite things was watching them give a trained ballroom dancer a hip-hop routine and seeing them nail it!

Learning to turn seemingly chaotic and uncomfortable situations into something spectacular is an attribute of great visionaries.

When things seem overwhelming, learn to dance your way out, one step at a time. Someone once asked me, "How do you eat an elephant?" My answer was, "One bite at a time." Sometimes we want things to happen quick, fast, and in a hurry. As years have gone by, I have learned that patience is indeed a virtue. What is meant for you will happen; it is just a matter of time – one dance step at a time.

ACTION ITEM: Name one thing you've always wanted to do. Today, take one small step toward that goal.

CONFESSION: I will not fret or worry. Instead of worrying, I will pray and let God know my concerns. Before I know it, a sense of God's wholeness, everything coming together for good, will come and settle me down.

POWER POINT
7

GOOD SUPPORT

Music supervisors place music in media such as movies, television shows, video games, and commercials. They work with studios, musicians, and their representatives to select appropriate music, and then secure the licenses to use it.

Teamwork is what the music supervisor relies on to help get his job done. He researches and scopes out talent that will help tell the story musically.

On your journey to fulfill your dreams, learning to interact with people should be a priority on your list of things to do. When I was in my early 20s, it was no problem to walk away from someone who did not share my all-knowing, perfect way of thinking. Later in life, I started learning the importance of relationships and treating others the way I prefer to be treated. People are valuable and should not be thrown away. Expand your capacity to give and receive.

Realizing that you are not the only gift that is being allowed to grace the earth brings one to a place of peace. Surrounding yourself with others who have similar drives and motivations only serves to strengthen you. Iron sharpens iron. It takes collaboration and a village to fulfill your dreams. An island needs dirt and water to be an island.

The goal is to build a team that moves in the same direction with the same acceleration. Moreover, use your gifts to support another's dreams. As a side note, if a person decides to leave your team or village, consider it an act of kindness. Keep moving.

ACTION ITEM: Today, evaluate your relationships. Is there someone you need to add to your team?

CONFESSION: My gifts and talents are not just for me. They will make room for me and bring me before great men.

POWER POINT
8
FOCUS FORWARD

A *focus puller* or *first assistant camera* or *1st AC*, is a part of the camera department. They are responsible for ensuring that the camera lens remains properly focused during shooting. They must pay close attention to the distance between actors and objects, and they must be able to judge how fast things move. Focus pullers must also be able to read the speed of light and know exactly what shutter speeds are needed to capture certain shots. Because of these responsibilities, focus pullers often end up working long hours and under extreme pressure.

The focus puller works side by side with the director of photography. Why is the focus puller a reminder of having a really good friend? Good question.

In order to fear less to do more, you need a good friend who can help you stay focused. When you're on your journey to fulfill your dreams, life throws curve balls that hit so hard and fast that it feels as though you're not in the game anymore. A good friend helps remind you of who you are and where you're going. A good friend pulls your focus. She or he helps you to see clearly and is willing to stay up long hours to listen and simply be there for you. Most importantly, a good friend is honest and not afraid to tell you hard truths in love. The right word at the right time places you in the right position—physically, emotionally, mentally, and spiritually.

Whenever you fall, consider that you have fallen forward. Every setback can be turned into a comeback. You don't have to stay down. Learn from the past, live in the present, and focus on the future. Focus forward knowing the best is yet to come.

> **ACTION ITEM**: Take the time to be a good friend.
>
> **CONFESSION**: God helped me to focus my eyes to see all the opportunities in front of me.

POWER POINT
9

BE TEACHABLE

A child actor working on a TV series or film during the school year will often need a certified *teacher* to provide instruction while on set.

There is a saying that teachers are students for life; they never stop learning. Learning is a part of their DNA and contributes to them being great at what they do. On your journey to fulfill your dreams, never stop learning about your craft, be willing to change with technology, and be open to new ways of serving your clients.

Technology is constantly changing: new ways of communicating, new cameras, new sound equipment, artificial intelligence, etc. Working at this production company decades ago, I remember one of my co-workers who had been at the company for a while and was great at what he did but rarely used the computer that sat in his office. He preferred to do everything by hand. One day I asked why he didn't use his computer. Turns out he was afraid of the technology. Eventually, he took a computer class for beginners and came out with more confidence. Like my co-worker, there are many who are afraid of technology and unfortunately become stagnated. Being like the teacher, always learning, is the key to not getting left behind.

Another key to following the ways of a teacher is learning to instruct in love and humility. Have you ever met a teacher that went to the dark side? Or, at least, that's what I call it. They become this self-proclaimed master and keeper of all knowledge and how it is distributed. They are the experts in all they survey. This group hides behind a so-called "passion for others to know the truth," as a way of excusing rude behavior. The truth is experts are needed, combined with sharing words of truth in love and humility.

> **ACTION ITEM**: Practice receiving and giving information in a strategic, productive way that benefits you and the other person.
>
> **CONFESSION:** I teach, and I learn.

POWER POINT
10

SEE IT. BELIEVE IT. DO IT.

Visual Effects is the process by which imagery is created or manipulated outside the context of a live-action

The power of visualization is being able to see it before it happens. A friend of mine showed me how he did the visual effects for a scene in Marvel's *Black Panther*. An object was thrown against a vehicle that made a dent—at least that's how it appears in the final scene. In reality, he and his team created the dent and placed the thrown object in the picture in post-production or editing. Prior to the scene being shot, they had to understand what the object would be and how it would make the impression on the metal. Let's just say a little science was involved.

There is power in visualization: seeing it before you see it. Then, moving forward to physically doing it—making the concept a physical reality. It's important to believe in yourself and your ability to do something bigger than yourself.

I learned about a three-step process that has been one of my favorite quotes, "What the mind can conceive and believe, and the heart desire, you can achieve." - Norman Vincent Peale The three-step process of believing, seeing, and achieving can be applied to any feat we want to accomplish.

> **ACTION ITEM:** Create and/or update your vision board.

CONFESSION: I will write my vision and make it plain so that others and I can understand and make it happen.

FINAL WORDS

Your dreams are much bigger than your fears. There is a dream you must manifest. Fear is a hindrance. Refuse to let it stop you. Coulda, Shoulda, and Woulda are triplets and such a waste of brain space. Fear *less* is what you do to do *more*. Insecurity is fear that is sometimes self-inflicted and can be influenced by others. On the other side of this wound is courage, confidence, and so much freedom!

Continue to remind yourself and practice the lessons in this book. You have what it takes to reach the level of success that is perfect for you. Move forward. You deserve everything good that's going to happen to you. Thank you for reading *Game Changer Playbook #1,10 Fear Less Do More Lessons* !

> "Let your dreams be bigger than your fears and your actions louder than your words."
> - M. Scott Peck

Here are key nuggets from each power point.

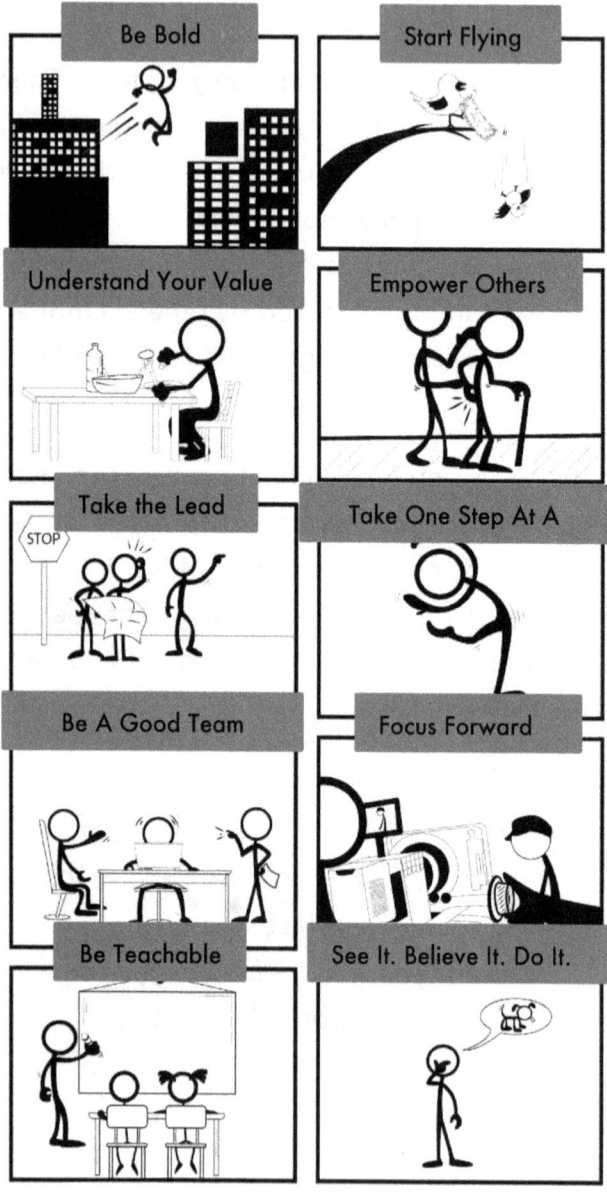

ACTION ITEMS

_____
_____
_____
_____
_____
_____
_____
_____
_____
_____
_____
_____
_____
_____
_____

"They may not see you coming, but they will know when you get there."
Tammy Adele Williams

GET ALL THREE PLAYBOOKS IN THE GAME CHANGER SERIES!

The Game Changer Series is a powerful three-book collection designed to help you break past fear, embrace change, and operate in your full potential!

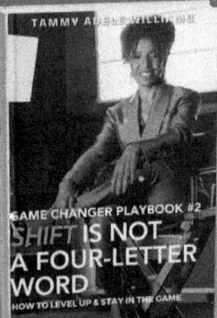

LOOK FOR OTHER GREAT BOOKS BY
TAMMY ADELE WILLIAMS

Order Today!

TAMMYDELEPUBLISHING.COM
amazon.com & where books are sold

Nnenia Knows Numbers is a vibrant, fun-filled counting book that celebrates the beauty and diversity of African American hairstyles. From one big afro to six tiny twists, each page introduces a new hairstyle, helping young readers practice their numbers while embracing cultural pride and self-love. With bold illustrations and rhythmic text, it's a joyful journey through styles as unique as the girls who wear them.

REFERENCES

PG. 9 A stunt performer is someone who performs dangerous stunts in a film or television production in place of an actor (*Collins Dictionary*)

PG. 18 A background actor or extra is a performer in a film, television show, stage, musical, opera, or ballet production, who appears in a nonspeaking or silent capacity, usually in the background (Wikipedia.com)

PG. 20 A choreographer is someone who invents the movements for a dance and tells the dancers how to perform them (*Collins Dictionary*)

PG. 28 Visual Effects is the process by which imagery is created or manipulated outside the context of a live action (Wikipedia)

PG 22 Music supervisors place music in media such as movies, television shows, video games, and commercials. They work with studios, musicians, and their representatives to select appropriate music, and then secure the licenses to use it (thebalance.com).

PG. 39 Visual Effects is the process by which imagery is created or manipulated outside the context of a live action (Wikipedia.com).

Biblical references: Holy Bible

www.ingramcontent.com/pod-product-compliance
Lightning Source LLC
Chambersburg PA
CBHW071958060426
42444CB00043B/2551